Who Am I?
Rainforest Animals

Written by Read With You
Center for Language Research and Development

Published by Read With You Publishing

Designed by Read With You Center for Language Research and Development

Read With You and associated logos are trademarks and/or registered trademarks of Read With You, LLC.

ISBN-13: 978-1-944710-83-5
ISBN-10: 1-944710-83-3

Printed in the United States of America.

I only poop once a week.

Who am I?

My big colorful bill is strong but light.

Who am I?

I'm a really good swimmer.

Who am I?

I use my eyes to help me swallow food.

Who am I?

I swing from branch to branch.

Who am I?

I'm one of the smartest birds.

Who am I?

I'm very poisonous.

Who am I?

My long tongue can reach both my eyes and ears.

Who am I?

Sloth

Toucan

Jaguar

Red-eyed Tree Frog

I am a sloth.

I am a toucan.

I am a jaguar.

I am a red-eyed tree frog.

Orangutan

Parrot

Poison Dart Frog

Okapi

I am an orangutan.

I am a parrot.

I am a poison dart frog.

I am an okapi.

We are rainforest animals.

A rainforest is a very dense, warm, and wet forest.